Reading 1

CAMBRIDGE SKILLS FOR FLUENCY

Cambridge Skills for Fluency is a series of supplementary materials covering the skills of listening, speaking, reading and writing; each skill is developed at four levels, from pre-intermediate through to upper-intermediate.

The series aims to develop students' confidence and fluency in English, by offering a variety of topics and activities which engage students' interest and encourage them to share their personal reactions and opinions.

Although all the books in the series share the same underlying principles, we have tried to avoid complete uniformity across the series, and so each book has its own features and its own particular approach to skills development:
- The *Listening* books aim to develop students' ability to understand real-life spoken English, through recordings of natural, spontaneous speech, selected and edited to make them accessible at each level.
- The *Speaking* books aim to develop oral fluency by focusing on topics that are personally relevant to students and which encourage students to draw on their own life experience, feelings and cultural knowledge.
- The *Reading* books aim to develop students' skill in reading English by introducing them to a wide variety of authentic texts, supported by tasks and activities designed to increase involvement and confidence in the reading process.
- The *Writing* books place writing in a central position in the language class, presenting it as a creative activity which contributes to language learning in general.

Level 1 of the series consists of the following titles:
Listening 1 by Adrian Doff and Carolyn Becket
Speaking 1 by Joanne Collie and Stephen Slater
Reading 1 by Simon Greenall and Diana Pye
Writing 1 by Andrew Littlejohn

CAMBRIDGE SKILLS FOR FLUENCY
Series Editor: Adrian Doff

Reading 1

Simon Greenall
Diana Pye

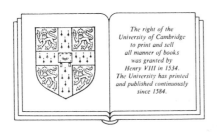

The right of the
University of Cambridge
to print and sell
all manner of books
was granted by
Henry VIII in 1534.
The University has printed
and published continuously
since 1584.

Cambridge University Press
Cambridge
New York   Port Chester
Melbourne   Sydney

Published by the Press Syndicate of the University of Cambridge
The Pitt Building, Trumpington Street, Cambridge CB2 1RP
40 West 20th Street, New York, NY 10011, USA
10 Stamford Road, Oakleigh, Melbourne 3166, Australia

© Cambridge University Press 1991

First published 1991

Printed in Great Britain
by Scotprint Ltd, Musselburgh, Scotland

ISBN 0 521 346711

GO

Contents

Map of the book

Unit	Function/Structural areas	Vocabulary areas	Reading strategies
1 Soft sell	Describing objects; describing people	Advertising	Extracting main ideas; linking ideas
2 Sleepless nights	Giving advice; describing processes	Sleep	Understanding text organisation; extracting main ideas; dealing with unfamiliar vocabulary
3 Tom's diner	Present continuous; saying what people are doing	Restaurants	Extracting main ideas; dealing with unfamiliar words; linking ideas
4 What's your line?	Present simple; talking about routine	Jobs	Predicting; extracting main ideas; reading for specific information; dealing with unfamiliar vocabulary
5 Poet's corner	Simple past	Nonsense poems	Extracting main ideas; dealing with unfamiliar words; understanding text organisation
6 Play it safe	Giving advice	Household accidents	Predicting; extracting main ideas; reading for specific information; dealing with unfamiliar words
7 A room with a view	Present continuous; describing what is happening; describing feelings	Paintings, feelings	Extracting main ideas; dealing with unfamiliar words
8 Excuses, excuses	Simple past; past continuous; telling stories	Rules and regulations	Extracting main ideas; dealing with unfamiliar words; understanding text organisation; linking ideas
9 Street furniture	Talking about obligation; prohibition; giving advice	Street signs, town facilities	Predicting; extracting main ideas; dealing with unfamiliar words

Unit	Function/Structural areas	Vocabulary areas	Reading strategies
10 How much do you like being with people?	Describing personal characteristics	Personal characteristics	Predicting; dealing with unfamiliar words; understanding text organisation
11 Brainteasers	Question forms: simple present		Reading for specific information; understanding text organisation; extracting main ideas
12 Women at work	Talking about abilities	Work, the office environment	Dealing with unfamiliar words; extracting main ideas; predicting; understanding text organisation
13 Getting through	Present simple; describing habit	Communication	Predicting; extracting main ideas; reading for specific information; linking ideas
14 Dads	Describing people; talking about ability	Family and relationships	Extracting main ideas; reading for specific information; dealing with unfamiliar words
15 What a mistake!	Past simple, past continuous		Extracting main ideas; dealing with unfamiliar words; linking ideas; understanding text organisation
16 Eating out		Food and drink	Extracting main ideas; understanding text organisation; dealing with unfamiliar words; linking ideas
17 Animal magic	Describing feelings, character	Animals, feelings, character	Predicting; extracting main ideas; dealing with unfamiliar words; linking ideas
18 Time off	Gerunds; talking about likes	Leisure activities	Predicting; understanding text organisation; dealing with unfamiliar words; reading for specific information
19 The Twenties	Simple past; talking about the past; making comparisons	Entertainment, shopping, transport, clothes, school	Extracting main ideas; dealing with unfamiliar words
20 Mini-sagas	Simple past		Extracting main ideas; dealing with unfamiliar words; linking ideas; understanding text organisation

Thanks

We are very grateful to the staff at the following schools and institutes who used the pilot editions and made so many useful comments: the Adult Migrant Education Service in Hobart and Melbourne, Australia; The Bell School in Cambridge; the British Institute in Rome; the British Schools in Rome and Florence; Eurocentre Cambridge; Eurocentre London (Lee Green); Footscray Adult Migrant Education Centre in Australia; Godmer House School of English in Oxford; the Istituto Tecnico Commerciale 'Maggiolini' in Parabiago (Milan); International House in Coimbra, Portugal; International House in Lisbon; LS Kieliopisto in Tampere, Finland; the Liceo Scientifico Statale 'Enriques' in Ostia (Rome); the London Study Centre; Klubschule Migros in Bern, Switzerland; the Studio School of English in Cambridge; the Université Lyon II in Lyon, France.

We would also like to thank our editors: Adrian Doff, Jeanne McCarten, Alison Baxter and Judith Aguda.

1 | Soft sell

1 Which word do you think is the most important in each of these advertisements?

a)

You've got to be quick to catch one.

b)

MINI

The cheeky

Mini.

Economical,

and glorious

fun to

drive

2 What does each advertisement say about the car?

1 It's a pleasure to drive.
2 It's not available for long.
3 It doesn't use much petrol.

4 It's fast.
5 It's a car for successful people.
6 It's the ideal town car.

3 Here are some other advertising slogans.

Put a tiger in your tank.
We'll take more care of you.
Let your fingers do the walking.
It's the real thing.

Match them with the products.

British Airways   Esso petrol
Coca Cola   Yellow Pages Telephone Directory

4 Think of a cigarette advertisement you know well. Is there a picture? What does it show?
What are the main colours? Are they important?
Are there any words? What do they tell you about the cigarettes?

5 Where could you see this advertisement? What is unusual about it?

Are you tired of looking at all these advertisements?

A bit dull, aren't they? How many more stations before you get off? How about something else to do while you wait?

Take a look at the person opposite you.
Don't stare! They might see you. And don't laugh!
What do you think they do for a living?
Do they like their job? What do they earn? More than you? Do they deserve to?
Do you think you could do their job? With one hand tied behind your back?
What do you think their first name is? What should it be? Think of a nickname.
Where do they live? What's their home like?
What's their favourite pastime? What paper do they read?
Where are they going now? And why? To meet somebody? Who?
And if they invited you to go out with them, what would you do?
Well, don't be too hard on this poor unsuspecting fellow-traveller.
Because there's another notice, just like this one, right above your head.

Well, that helped pass the time, didn't it? Now, is this your station?

Thank you for travelling with us.
HELP KEEP LONDONERS UNDERGROUND.

6 Choose three words from the advertisement which you do not understand.
Can you guess what they mean? You can use your dictionary to check.

7

Who or *what*? Answer these questions about words in the advertisement.

1 'What do you think *they* do for a living?' Who are *they*?
2 'What should *it* be?' What is *it*?
3 '. . . on this *poor unsuspecting fellow traveller*, . . .' Who and where is this traveller?
4 '. . . just like *this one*, . . . ' Which one?

8

Look at one of the people below. Just a quick glance. Try not to stare. Answer the questions in the advertisement in exercise 5.

9

Are there advertisements in your country for:

– a car?
– an airline?
– petrol?
– perfume?
– a drink?

Think about one of these advertisements. What does it tell you about the product? What picture does it show? What does the slogan say?

2 | Sleepless nights

1 **Do you ever find it difficult to get to sleep? What do you do? Do you ever:**

- read a boring book?
- count sheep?
- practise your English?
- make an anagram of: *I want to go to sleep?*
- do mental arithmetic?
- do the housework?
- write an important letter?
- put your finger in your ear?
- take a sleeping tablet?
- get up and make a cup of tea?

Can you think of any other things to do?

2 **The pictures opposite show someone making a cup of tea in the middle of the night, but they are in the wrong order. Match the sentences with the pictures.**

1 Go out of room, down corridor (creep). Find door handle. Open door.
2 Fill kettle. Wait for it to boil.
3 Get up and bump into things in dark. Stub toe. Sssssh!
4 Wake up. Pour away cold tea. Make another cup.
5 Stub toe on bed again and spill tea over bedclothes.
6 Find kitchen. Turn on light. Look for tea. Look for cup under washing up. Do not make noise with dirty crockery.
7 Pour water on tea. Wait for it to brew. Fall asleep.
8 A cup of tea would be nice. I think I'll definitely get myself one in a minute.
9 Add milk and sugar to taste. Pick tea up. Leave kitchen. Return to bedroom.
10 Switch on light. Oooops! Wrong door. Leave toilet. Go to kitchen.

HOW TO MAKE A CUP OF TEA IN 2½ HOURS

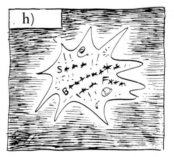

3 Put the pictures and sentences in order.

4 Underline the words or phrases which helped you match the sentences to the pictures.

5 What is the main idea of the story? Choose the best sentence.

1 Ordinary activities can be extremely difficult at night.
2 People living alone have special habits and routines.
3 You can't help making a lot of noise at night.
4 There's never a clean cup when you make tea at night.

6 Write down in your own language what you think these words mean. Use the pictures to help you.

kettle   boil   bump   stub   spill   crockery   brew

You can use a dictionary to check.

7 This passage is about what people often do when they are asleep. Where do these words go? You can use one word twice.

snore	snoring
talk	talking
walk	walker
wake up	walkers

Sometimes people sit up in bed and shout! Some people (1) .... in their sleep, repeating phrases they used during the day, or (2) .... nonsense. These people rarely remember what they have said next morning.

Occasionally a person may (3) .... while they are asleep. Sleep (4) .... move clumsily, bumping into furniture. Their eyes may be open but glazed, and they may mutter to themselves. Unless they (5) ...., they rarely remember anything about it the next day. Waking up a sleep (6) .... will not harm him.

But apart from dreaming, the most common sleeping activity is (7) .... (8) .... usually disturbs other people but not the sleeper, although some people (9) .... so loudly that they wake themselves up too. The only way to stop someone is to wake them up.

Do you or anyone in your family do any of these things? What can you do to stop them?

6

3 | Tom's diner

1   A *diner* is a type of restaurant in the United States of America. In the pictures, can you see anyone:

- sitting at a table?
- pouring coffee?
- kissing someone?
- talking?
- eating?

- hitching up her skirt?
- reading a newspaper?
- looking out of the window?
- straightening her stockings?
- doing the washing up?

You can use your dictionary or ask your teacher for help.

a)

b)

2   What are the differences between the two pictures?

Example: *In picture (a), the woman is sitting alone but in picture (b) she is with a friend.*

3 Read the song. Which picture shows what is happening?

Tom's Diner

I am sitting
In the morning
At the diner
On the corner

5 I am waiting
At the counter
For the man
To pour the coffee

And he fills it
10 Only halfway
And before
I even argue

He is looking
Out the window
15 At somebody
Coming in

'It is always
Nice to see you'
Says the man
20 Behind the counter

To the woman
Who has come in
She is shaking
Her umbrella

25 And I look
The other way
As they are kissing
Their hellos

I'm pretending
30 Not to see them
And instead
I pour the milk

I open
Up the paper
35 There's a story
Of an actor

Who had died
While he was drinking
It was no one
40 I had heard of

And I'm turning
To the horoscope
And looking
For the funnies

When I'm feeling   45
Someone watching me
And so
I raise my head

There's a woman
On the outside   50
Looking inside
Does she see me?

No she does not
Really see me
'Cause she sees   55
Her own reflection

And I'm trying
Not to notice
That she's hitching
Up her skirt   60

And while she's
Straightening her stockings
Her hair
Has gotten wet

Oh, this rain   65
It will continue
Through the morning
As I'm listening

To the bells
Of the cathedral   70
I am thinking
Of your voice

And of the midnight picnic
Once upon a time
Before the rain began . . .   75

And I finish up my coffee
It's time to catch the train

(Suzanne Vega)

4 Write down in your own language what you think these words from the song mean.

  corner   counter   funnies   reflection   midnight   picnic

Check in your dictionary.

5 Are these statements about the song true or false?

  1 It's a bright and sunny day.
  2 The singer is having dinner.
  3 The man works at Tom's Diner.
  4 The woman who comes in does not know the man well.
  5 The woman outside is concerned about how she looks.
  6 The singer is thinking about someone she knows well.
  7 The singer is waiting to take a train.

6 Read these lines from the song. Who do the words in *italics* refer to?

  1 *He* is looking / Out the window / At *somebody* / Coming in (lines 13–16)
  2 Who had died / While *he* was drinking (lines 37–38)
  3 *She* is shaking / Her umbrella (lines 23–24)
  4 No *she* does not / Really see *me* (lines 53–54)
  5 'It is always / Nice to see *you*' (lines 17–18)
  6 I am thinking / Of *your* voice (lines 71–72)

7 Which is the best summary of the song?

  1 A woman is reading a newspaper while she is having coffee in a diner when she sees the man behind the counter kissing a woman who has just come in. Outside another woman is using the window as a mirror. The first woman finishes her coffee and leaves.

  2 A woman is having coffee in a diner because it is raining. She is very interested in what everyone else is doing, but she pretends that she is reading a newspaper. She leaves to get her train.

  3 A woman is waiting to catch her train. She is leaving town after the end of a relationship. As she drinks her coffee, she is watching what other people are doing, but she cannot stop herself from thinking about her ex-boyfriend.

8 Read the song again and write down the ten most important words.
Does the song have a happy or a sad ending?
Imagine that this is not the end of the song. How do you think it continues?

9

4 | What's your line?

1 What are these people doing? What job do you think they do?

a)

b)

c)

2 Read the three passages opposite.

Match each passage with one of the pictures.
What jobs do the people do? Choose from this list.

priest	bus driver	farmer	postman
teacher	storyteller	actor	doctor

10

1   Here on Skye I do more than deliver letters and parcels. There aren't any buses or trains on this part of the island, so the post office also runs a passenger service. The bus which I drive has eleven seats so people from the farms and villages can get into Broadford for shopping or for work.

I live in Elgol, a small village on the south-west coast of the island. I leave Elgol post office every morning at 8 a.m. and drive my bus 24km. to Broadford. I stop for passengers and empty the five post boxes along the road.

I also pick up the school children that live along my route and take them to the school in Broadford. There's a school for young children in Elgol, but the older children have to travel into the town.

Sometimes it takes me about three hours to finish my round. I take shopping to some of the elderly people who can't always get to Broadford; I deliver the milk and newspapers six days a week. I shouldn't deliver animals, but I sometimes take a puppy or a rabbit as a passenger. The Post Office charges people, of course, for all these extra services. It's 70p to travel from Elgol to Broadford and it costs 10p to deliver a pint of milk.

People often ask me how I like living here on Skye, especially since I come from the city. Well, it's difficult to explain, but here I feel part of the community; it's good to know that you are helping people. I'd hate to live in the city again.

2   I enjoy my work, especially here in the suburbs. There are two churches here: I preach in both of them. The new church has also got a number of meeting rooms. There we have Sunday school – well, actually it's on Saturdays over here – for the younger children and social meetings for the older children. At the moment I'm trying to start a youth club.

Female priests are unusual in many other countries. Here in Denmark they are becoming more common now. At the moment 12 per cent of Denmark's priests are women. But traditionally it's a man's job, and some religious groups still refuse to recognise female priests. I don't understand exactly why some people are afraid of female priests.

Women are often more in touch with things than men. After all, they're mothers and housewives like other women, and often it's easier to talk with a woman about your problems than it is with a man. So I think that there should be male and female priests in every parish.

3   This is a very old job in China, and today there are still tens of thousands of us who do it. You can often see us on street corners in the summer evenings, surrounded by children.

My mother taught me to be honest and kind through stories, and I began to tell them to children sixty years ago, when I was a young teacher. I retired in 1966 and now I tell them at children's cultural centres and schools.

I listen to the words children use and learn what makes them laugh when they're playing street games. You must learn to talk their language. Stories are the best way of teaching moral lessons to young people. But many of my stories are also about people in other countries, so I read a lot. I talk about the Tower of London, for example, and then about the lives of people in England today. If children don't like a story they show it, so I try them first with kids who live nearby.

Every morning I go to the park near my home with a lot of other elderly people to do Tai'Chi. After breakfast, I listen to the radio and then read a lot, write stories – and tell them.

3 Match these introductions with the passages.

A Sun Jingxiu, an 80-year-old retired teacher, is the oldest storyteller in the country. He lives in a flat in Beijing with his youngest son, his daughter-in-law, and his four-year-old granddaughter.

B The Reverend Elisabeth Lyneborg, aged 42, is the vicar of Farum, a suburb of Copenhagen. She became a priest six years ago and now has a busy life looking after her parish and her five children.

C Nigel Nice is 31 and a postman on Skye, an island off the west coast of Scotland. He lives in the small village of Elgol, which is 24 km from the nearest town.

4 Complete the chart below.

Name	Nigel Nice		Elisabeth Lyneborg
Place of work		Beijing, China	
Job	postman		priest
Duties		writes and tells stories on street corners, visits schools and cultural centres, teaches moral lessons	

5 Try to imagine the village of Elgol in the first passage in exercise 2. Which of these sentences do you think are true?

1 It's on the coast.
2 It's very small.
3 It's got several shops.
4 It's got a school.
5 There are farms around the village.
6 People don't pay for the extra services.

6 Look at the second passage in exercise 2 again. Choose the best meanings for
these words.

suburb: a) a district outside the centre of town
               b) the centre of town   c) the country

preach: a) work very hard   b) give a religious talk   c) lead

recognise: a) know   b) meet   c) accept

parish: a) the district around a church   b) a village
               c) a town with a cathedral

7 Look at passage 3 again. Complete this summary of the passage.

If you go into town on a summer evening, you may see a (1) .... in the
street. The stories often teach (2) .... lessons to young people. They
are also a good way of teaching children about life in (3) .... Sun
Jingxiu believes that to be a good storyteller you need to (4) .... and
(5) ....

8 Which is the most unusual of these three jobs? Why?
Is there any job you would like to do? Why?

5 | Poet's corner

The passages in this unit are all *nonsense poems*.

1 What is the best title for these poems?

Mr Nobody   Honey   One Day
The Duel   Days   Who's there?

1 As I was coming down the stair
  I met a man who wasn't there;
  He wasn't there again today:
  I wish that man would go away.

2 I eat peas with honey,
  I've done it all my life:
  It makes the peas taste funny,
  But it keeps them on the knife.

3 As I was going out one day
  My head fell off and rolled away.
  But when I saw that it was gone
  I picked it up and put it on.

  And when I got into the street
  A fellow cried 'Look at your feet!'
  I looked at them and sadly said:
  'I've left them both asleep in bed.'

4 One fine day in the middle of the night
  Two dead men got up to fight,
  Two blind men to see fair play,
  Two dumb men to shout 'Hurray!'
  And two lame men to carry them away.

2 What do these words mean? You can use your own language.

stair   peas   honey   rolled away   picked up
fight   blind   dumb   lame

You can use your dictionary or ask your teacher for help.

3 In each poem, there are some strange or impossible ideas. Can you say what they are?

4 The poems below are *limericks*. Read them aloud. Can you say what is special about a limerick? Which one do you like best?

There was an old man of Peru
Who dreamt he was eating his shoe;
    He woke in the night
    In a terrible fright,
And found it was perfectly true.

There was a Young Lady of Riga
Who rode with a smile on a tiger;
    They returned from the ride
    With the lady inside,
And the smile on the face of the tiger.

There was a young man of St Just
Who ate apple pie till he bust;
    It wasn't the fruit
    That caused him to do it,
What finished him off was the crust.

There was an old lady of Wye
Who was baked by mistake in a pie;
    To the household's disgust
    She emerged through the crust,
And exclaimed with a yawn 'Where am I?'

There once was a man of Bengal
Who was asked to a fancy dress ball;
    He murmured, 'I'll risk it
    And go as a biscuit',
But a dog ate him up in the hall.

There was a small maiden named Maggie
Whose dog was enormous and shaggy
    The front end of him
    Looked vicious and grim,
But the tail end was friendly and waggy.

There was a young lady of Twickenham
Whose boots were too tight to walk quick in them;
    She wore them a while
    But at last with a smile,
She pulled them both off and was sick in them.

5   Here are two poems about noses. Can you separate them? The lines are in the right order.

> Oh, what a thing is a nose!
> It doesn't breathe;
> It doesn't smell;
> It grows and it grows and it grows,
> It doesn't feel
> So very well.
> I am discouraged
> With my nose:
> The only thing it
> It grows on your head
> While you're lying in bed
> Does is blows.
> At the opposite end to your toes.

6   Read the poems in this unit again. Which do you like best? Which do you like least? Why? Which poems do you think are:

- obscure?   – funny?   – silly?
- clever?   – ridiculous?   – strange?

7   Do you have nonsense poems in your own language? What kind of poetry do you like to read in your own language?

6 | Play it safe

Four children are killed by accidents every day.

Accidents are the commonest cause of death among children.

One in every six children in hospital is there because of an accident.

1 Do you know anyone (a child or an adult) who has had an accident at home? What sort of accident was it?
In your own language, write down five accidents that can happen to children in the home.

2 Match the pictures with the passages on page 18.

a)

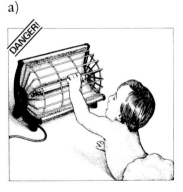

b)

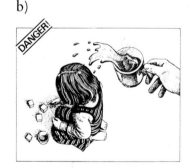

c)

d)

e)

1   **Scalds**

Small children don't understand that hot water and hot drinks can be dangerous. We often forget the dangers ourselves. Yet it only takes a cup of hot tea or coffee or a bath that's too hot to scald a child badly. A severe scald can mean a long stay in hospital, and a really severe scald can kill.

2   **Falls**

Children of all ages fall and hurt themselves from time to time. Luckily most falls aren't serious, but some can cause severe injuries, such as head injuries.

For babies, the danger is rolling off the edge of something like a bed, chair, table or kitchen worktop.

Toddlers soon learn to climb and explore. To them, climbing on furniture doesn't seem dangerous. It's just fun. But it's very easy for a toddler to fall off a piece of furniture, or down the stairs, or even out of a window or off a balcony.

With older children, adventure accidents are a problem. Climbing trees, high walls, or fences can be dangerous.

3   **Burns**

Every year children die in house fires and many more are badly burnt. A cigarette, for example, can easily start a fire. And many fires are started by children playing with matches.

But of course it's not only fires that cause burns. There are things in every home that can burn a child badly – a hot iron, for example, or an electric fire.

4   **Drowning**

Children love playing with water. Whether it's in the bath at bed time or in the garden pond or in the sea, water is fun. But it is also dangerous. A baby or toddler can drown in very shallow water – far less than you put in the bath.

5   **Cuts**

Glass causes the most serious cuts. Few people realise just how serious glass cuts are. Yet every year about 7,000 children end up in hospital because of accidents with glass. These are not only accidents with things like broken bottles. More often the children have fallen through a glass door or window and are badly hurt.

18

3 Look at the following words.

scald   fall   burn   drowning   cut

Now look at the words in context. What other words help you understand their meaning? Write them down.

Example: Scald – *hot + water, drinks, tea, coffee; a bath that's too hot.*

4 Look again at the five accidents you wrote down in exercise 1. How many of them are mentioned in the text?

5 Read the passages again and say what could cause the following accidents. Fill in the chart.

Burns	Scalds	Cuts	Falls	Drowning
cigarettes	hot tea	glass doors	stairs	garden pond

6 Say what accident each piece of advice may prevent.
Example: Don't carry hot drinks over a child's head. – *scalds*

How to prevent accidents

1 Fit a safety gate at the top of stairs.
2 Make sure your children learn to swim as early as possible.
3 If your child wears glasses, ask for plastic lenses.
4 Always put cold water in the bath first.
5 Don't put furniture near upstairs windows.
6 Keep matches and lighters well out of children's reach.
7 Don't carry hot drinks over a child's head.
8 Use special safety fireguards in front of all fires.
9 Don't let a toddler walk around holding anything made of glass.
10 Make sure toys have no sharp edges or points.
11 Never leave a baby or toddler alone in a bath for one second.
12 Fit locks on upstairs windows.
13 Never smoke in bed.
14 Don't leave young children alone when they're near or in water.
15 Don't drink anything hot with a child on your lap.

7 Think of these sports.

horse riding   cycling
mountaineering   sailing
skiing   deep-sea diving

What accidents might happen? How could you prevent them?

7 | A room with a view

1

Put the titles with the paintings.
(There are some extra titles.)

A Passing Storm
The Card Players
Room in New York
The Dance of Life
The Family Reunion
A Day by the Sea

1

2

3

2 Which statements do you think describe what is happening in the pictures?

Painting 1
a) The man and his wife have nothing to say to each other.
b) The two people are very busy.
c) Time is passing very slowly.

Painting 2
a) The storm outside is over.
b) The two people are strangers.
c) The couple have just had an argument.

Painting 3
a) The two women are waiting for friends.
b) The two women are waiting for someone to invite them to dance.
c) The woman in the dark dress has been waiting for a long time.

3 Look at the people in the paintings. Do you think they feel:

- lonely?   - cynical?
- happy?   - worried?
- sad?   - bored?
- optimistic?   - angry?
- pessimistic?

You can use a dictionary or ask your teacher for help.

How do they feel about each other?
What do you think will happen to them?

4 Match the descriptions opposite with the paintings.

5 Look at the words in *italics*. Do you know what they mean? Can you guess? Check with your dictionary.

6 Write down five words or phrases from each passage which best describe the atmosphere and meaning of the painting it describes.

A ... The couple have clearly had an argument, but the title of the painting suggests that it will soon be over.

James Tissot was a Frenchman who lived for many years in England at a time when pictures which tell a story were very popular. In this picture the *background* explains what the *figures* have done and are about to do. There is a storm over the harbour outside, which suggests that there is a storm indoors also; and the clearer sky tells us that the *quarrel* has finished.

This painting is attractive for its details – the tea-service, the dress, the balcony and the ship in the distance.

B ... The two young women are watching people dancing, and waiting for an invitation to join in. But we can see no one who is likely to make this invitation, since all the men are already dancing with partners. The woman on the left is still hopeful and the colours of her dress suggest this; perhaps she has only just arrived. The woman on the right is more realistic. Perhaps she has had to wait too long, or maybe she is more experienced. Her dark dress reflects a view of life which is much less *optimistic*. She stands there, lonely and sad.

Munch's early life was unhappy. He was afraid of life and unlucky in love. His paintings are full of symbolism which reflect this. In this painting, we have a view of life which moves from left to right, from fresh hope through worldly experience to *cynicism* and disgust.

C ... the American seems to look at his newspaper only because he cannot think of anything better to do. He is home from work, but has nothing to say to his wife; she turns away, and plays a note or two on the piano.

The artist often walked along the streets of New York at night, and sometimes saw rooms like this one, with people inside who did not know that he was watching them. The window is a major part of his painting, and the artist seems to show two ordinary people in a typical moment of their separate and unexciting lives.

Many of Edward Hopper's pictures suggest loneliness: isolated buildings with no sign of life, or *shabby* rooms in hotels or cafés in which one or two people stare ahead of them. The couple in this picture are sitting only a few feet apart, but no longer enjoy each other's company. Each thinks his or her own thoughts, and waits for time to pass.

7 Do you like the paintings? Would you like them in your home? If so, where would you put them? Why?

8 Think of a title for this picture.

Its real title is in the list in exercise 1. Can you find it?
What can you see and what do the people feel? Write a few sentences describing it.

8 | Excuses, excuses

ex·cuse /ɪkˈskjuːs/ *n* reason given (true or false) to explain what one has done; apology: *He's always making excuses for being late.*

1
Here are some situations when you may have to make excuses.

driving too fast
arriving late for work or school
having an accident in your car
not paying your taxes
not replying to letters
not going to a wedding

What excuses can you make?

2
**Have you ever been in any of these situations? What excuse did you make?
Can you remember any other situations when you had to make an excuse?**

25

3 In the following situations the excuses are missing. Can you think of an excuse for each situation?

1 A Brentford man was fined £2, for riding a bicycle without care. When he was arrested, he was riding without his hands on the handlebars, reading a newspaper. The man told the court . . .

2 Arriving at the factory 90 minutes late, a worker apologised for the delay with the excuse that his alarm clock was 30 minutes slow. 'But what happened to the other 60 minutes?' asked the man's boss . . .

3 The famous Dorothy Parker was ready with a quick, if simple, excuse when asked by the editor of *The New Yorker* why she sat staring into space instead of getting on with some writing . . .

4 The police asked a driver from Glasgow why he had not told them in writing that he had sold his car. The driver replied . . .

5 A worker arrived late yet again one morning and, really desperate for an excuse, he blamed his late arrival on the World Cup Final between England and West Germany . . .

4 Choose excuses for the situations from the list.

a) 'Because somebody else is using the pencil.'
b) 'My pen didn't have much ink, and I needed what was left to fill in a new dog licence.'
c) 'Sorry I ran over the dog, but I was trying to avoid a cat.'
d) 'I was dreaming about the game and, as it went into extra time, I had to stay asleep until the end of the match.'
e) 'I would have gone, but it looked like rain.'
f) 'It's the only chance I ever get to read a newspaper.'
g) 'A pedestrian hit me and went right under the car.'
h) 'Well, I spent an hour trying to find a phone that worked so I could ring you to tell you I'd be a little late this morning.'
i) 'They've just put up the price, and I didn't have enough on me.'
j) 'While sitting on the train I was shocked to notice that I had a blue sock on one foot and a yellow one on the other, so I had to go home to change them.'
k) 'I wanted something fresh to eat while I was in Britain.'

Did you think of any similar excuses in exercise 3?

5   What do these words mean? You can use your own language.

fined
dog licence
handlebars
pedestrian
blamed
shocked
really desperate

You can use a dictionary to check.

6   Look again at the extra excuses in exercise 4. Think of situations when you could use them.

7   Read the three stories and complete them with these sentences.

a) The judge was not impressed.
b) He let the driver go.
c) I am a music lover.
d) Soon there was a police car behind him.
e) She had the perfect reply.

A   Police stopped a driver who had not reported an accident. The *man* said *he* had no knowledge about backing his car into another car, which was not moving, and setting off the burglar alarm. (1) '.................................... I was listening to a Mozart clarinet concerto on the car radio. *I* thought the alarm was simply a badly played note.' Fortunately the judge was a music lover too. (2) ....

B   A motorist left the automatic car wash and drove down the road at 60 miles an hour. (3) .... When they stopped him, he explained, 'I was driving faster than usual to let the wind blow water from off the roof so it wouldn't collect on the windscreen.'

C   A judge in Sacramento, California asked a woman why *she* had appeared before *him* in court 24 times for driving too fast. (4) .... 'I'm so sorry, sir. I'm afraid I've fallen in love with *you* and I don't know how else I can see you. Will you give me your photograph?' (5) .... He fined *her* £100 and took away her driving licence for a year.

8   Who do the words in *italics* refer to?

9 Which is the most *creative* story? Why do you think so?

10 What creative excuses can you make for these situations?

You have forgotten the meaning of a word you learnt during the last lesson.
You have to leave your class early today.
You have forgotten to return a friend's book.
You have left your English homework at your house.

9 | Street furniture

1   Look at the title and the photos in this unit. What do you think 'street furniture' is? Give some examples. What do you think the photographs show?

2   Where can you see these signs? Choose from the list below.

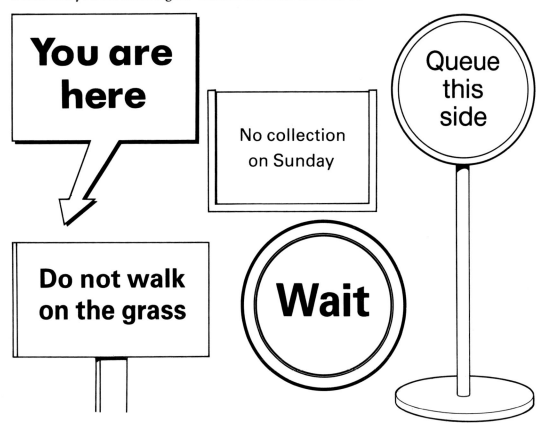

bench   bus stop
post box   pedestrian crossing with traffic lights
drinking fountain   street map
park

3 a)

b)

c)

d)

e)

What items of street furniture do the passages describe? Read them and match them with the photographs.

1 In towns, there were very few bus shelters until about thirty years ago. Since then they have appeared everywhere, probably because most people no longer wear the kinds of clothes that protect them from the wind, cold and rain. Country bus shelters have been with us for a good deal longer. Before the Second World War, many of them were paid for by rich local people, often in memory of a member of their family. Some were well built and very attractive, to fit in with the surroundings.

2 By the 1870's public lavatories were being installed all over Britain. Many of them, for gentlemen only, were made of iron, highly decorated and often in the shape of Indian or Greek temples. A little later, in the 1880's, more solid structures of brick or stone were being built, with accommodation for ladies and gentlemen. Some of these looked like cottages or medieval castles.

3 Public drinking fountains are to be found everywhere. Most of them were built in the nineteenth century and some are very grand. The old type of drinking fountain was not very hygienic. It usually had an iron drinking cup, fixed to a chain, and everyone used it. They were built for three reasons. Firstly, they provided people with pure water to drink, at a time when much of the drinking water available, especially from wells and pumps, was dangerous to health. Secondly, they were memorials to local residents. Finally, they were intended to persuade people to drink water, instead of beer or spirits.

4 **Choose the best meanings for these words.**

protect: Clothes that protect you against the bad weather are clothes which: (a) let in the wind, cold and rain. (b) keep you warm and dry.

rural: The paragraph describes town bus shelters and rural ones. Rural is likely to mean: (a) town. (b) country.

erected: The paragraph describes when and why public drinking fountains were erected. It means: (a) built. (b) decorated.

memorial: One reason for building the drinking fountain was as a memorial for someone who lived nearby. So a memorial here is probably something: (a) to help you remember someone who is dead. (b) to provide fresh drinking water.

5 Read each passage again and fill in the chart.

	Bus shelters	Public lavatories	Fountains
Why were they built?	to protect people from bad weather	—	
When were the first ones built?			
What are they made of?	—		—
What do they look like?			

6 Some street furniture tells us about life in the past. From the passages, say how people lived in the past.

Example: *They didn't have clean water.*

7 What street furniture do you have in your country? What does it tell us about life in your country?

10 | How much do you like being with people?

1 Look at the two photographs. What do you think the people are like? Here are some useful words.

entertaining	interesting	friendly	reliable
relaxed	honest	understanding	happy

a)

b)

2 All these words describe personality. Which are positive? Which are negative? You can look up any words you do not understand in your dictionary.

entertaining	interesting	pleasant	dull	boring
friendly	unhappy	unpleasant	honest	happy
unfriendly	reliable	tense	dishonest	relaxed
uninteresting	unreliable			

3 These sentences are missing from the questionnaire. Decide where they go.

i) Someone who makes you happy.
ii) Join in?
iii) Generally you can get on with almost anyone?
iv) Because they like you?
v) Years, usually.

1 Last time you had friends over, was it:
   a) Because you find them entertaining and interesting?
   b) ....
   c) Because you thought you had to?

2 When you are on holiday, do you:
   a) Usually make friends easily?
   b) Prefer to spend time alone?
   c) Want to make friends, but find it difficult?

3 You have arranged to meet a friend but are very tired.
   When you are unable to phone him/her, do you?
   a) Not turn up, hoping that he/she will understand?
   b) Turn up and try to enjoy yourself?
   c) Turn up but go home early?

4 How long do you keep your friends?
   a) ....
   b) It varies; with something in common, it can be for
      years.
   c) Not long; you usually find new friends.

5 Do you usually make friends:
   a) Through people you already know?
   b) In many different ways?
   c) Only after a long time and with some difficulty?

6 What kind of person do you choose for a friend?
   a) ....
   b) Someone who is reliable.
   c) Someone who is interested in you.

7 Which statement describes you best?
   a) I usually make people laugh.
   b) I usually make people think.
   c) People feel relaxed with me.

8 If you are asked to join in a game or sing at a party,
   do you:
   a) Make an excuse to get out of it?
   b) Join in with pleasure?
   c) ....

9 Which statement is true for you?
   a) I like to say pleasant things about my friends.
   b) I'm very honest; I sometimes have to say unpleasant
       things about them.
   c) I do not praise or criticize my friends.

10 Do you find that:
   a) You can get on well only with people who have the
       same interests?
   b) ....
   c) Sometimes you try to get on with someone who is
       unfriendly?

4 **Now answer the questionnaire.**

   How much do you like being with people? Here is the answer key.

1 a:3	b:2	c:1	**6** a:3	b:2	c:1
2 a:3	b:2	c:1	**7** a:2	b:1	c:3
3 a:1	b:3	c:2	**8** a:2	b:3	c:1
4 a:3	b:2	c:1	**9** a:3	b:1	c:2
5 a:2	b:3	c:1	**10** a:1	b:3	c:2

   If your total score is:
   26–30, you like people very much and enjoy life.
   21–25, you are friendly, but sometimes like to be alone.
   15–20, you probably like to spend a lot of time alone.

5 **What types of word do these endings suggest? (nouns, verbs, adjectives and
   so on)**

   -y   -ly   -ily   -ed   -ing   -able

   They may suggest more than one type of word.
   **Find examples of words with these endings in the questionnaire. What type
   of word is each one?**

6

Read the description of Woody Allen, the actor and film director. Can you find four words or expressions which describe his personality?

Where was Woody on Oscar Night? Playing the clarinet like any other Monday evening. Even if the Oscar ceremony had taken place on another night, he probably would not have gone. He is a small, complicated, extremely shy man who always keeps himself to himself. To avoid being recognised in the street he either hides inside his big Parka hood or wears a variety of disguises. He is fond of humanity but does not feel at ease with people.

How would Woody Allen answer the questionnaire?

11 | Brainteasers

1 **What is a brainteaser? (Do not worry if you don't know. You will soon find out!)**
First, can you find the names of two countries which are hidden in each sentence below?
Example: *Vladimir and Olga are Soviet names.*

1 Have you ever heard an animal talk in dialect?
2 Evening classes may help an amateur to improve his painting.
3 If your exhaust pipe rusts you just have to shrug and accept it.
4 In letters to the press we denounce the wholesale ban on luxury imports.
5 Such a display could be either grand or rather vulgar.

2 **Put the words in order and make quotations.**

1 names their enemies forget forgive never your but
2 moments awful some but hours has half Wagner some wonderful
3 and early man bed a to wealthy rise early makes to healthy dead and
4 your middle show age around begins is when age middle your to

3 Match questions to answers.

1 What question can you never answer Yes to?
2 What occurs once in a minute, twice in a moment, but not once in a hundred years?
3 What time is it when the clock strikes thirteen?
4 What do you find in the middle of Glasgow?
5 What word do people always pronounce incorrectly?
6 What letter is useful to a deaf woman?
7 What is it that everyone thinks is always coming but never really arrives?
8 What is it that you can't hold for half an hour, even though it's lighter than a feather?
9 What is the one thing you break when you name it?
10 What is always in front of you, even though you can never see it?
11 What goes from New York to Philadelphia but never moves?
12 With what can you fill a barrel to make it lighter than when it is empty?

a) The future.
b) Silence.
c) The letter S.
d) Tomorrow.
e) The letter A because it makes *her hear*.
f) Time to get a new clock.
g) The motorway.
h) Your breath.
i) Holes.
j) The letter M.
k) Are you asleep?
l) The word *incorrectly*.

4 What do these words mean? You can use a dictionary.

occurs   strikes   incorrectly   deaf   feather   barrel

5 Copy and punctuate the brainteasers.

a farmer was asked how many animals he had he answered theyre all horses except for two all sheep except for two and all pigs except for two how many animals did he have

a son asked his father how old he was and the father replied your age is now one quarter of mine but five years ago it was only one-fifth how old is the father

Can you solve them?

6 Here are some more brainteasers. Can you solve these?

1 A man can eat ten kilos of cheese in twenty days, but if his wife shares it they can finish it in fourteen days. How long would it take his wife to eat the cheese alone?

2 Lady Constance met the Countess of Kensington in the dining room. 'Don't I know you?' asked Lady Constance. 'You certainly ought to,' replied the Countess. 'Your mother was my mother's only daughter.' How are they related?

3 If you had a five-litre container and a three-litre container, how could you measure out one litre of liquid?

4 When you see the reflection of a clock in a mirror and the time appears to be 2.30, what time is it really?

5 When asked her age, Aunt Agatha replied that she was 35 years old, not counting Saturdays and Sundays. What was her real age?

6 Johnny, Willy and Bobby were fishing by the river when suddenly someone on the other bank fired a gun. Johnny saw the smoke rising from the gun, Willy saw the bullet hit the water with a splash and Bobby heard the gun go off with a bang. Which of the three boys knew about the shot first?

7 **Here are some logic puzzles. Can you solve them?**

1

John's free time is spent fishing,
   Mr Smith plays golf.
David Brown does not go swimming,
   Nor does Mr Rolfe.
Who's the person keen on bowling?
   Which is Mr Andy Sheene?

Peter's hobby is canoeing –
   He's not Mr Green.
Mr Green is not the swimmer,
   Nor is his pal Bobby.
Now you can decide their names.
   Which is Mr Sheene's hobby?

Name	Hobby

2 Three friends, Amelia, Bernice and Caroline are having lunch in a
   restaurant. Amelia is older than the redhead but younger than the
   hairdresser. Bernice is younger than the blonde, and Caroline is older than
   the brunette. The typist is the receptionist's younger sister. Can you give
   the hair colour and occupation of each girl in order of age?

Name	Colour of hair	Occupation
(youngest)		
(oldest)		

12 | Women at work

1 **Look at the following cartoons. Is the person in each picture a man or a woman? Why do you think so?**

2 What do the pictures show? How could you use these words to talk about them?

an accident   a cluttered desk   hard worker   burnt   important
a busy office   a business meeting   family   married   boss
company   a chaotic kitchen   well organised   dangerous
responsible   career

You can look up any words you do not understand in your dictionary.

3 Read this poem by N. Josefowitz. Which picture in exercise 1 shows a situation described in the poem?

Impressions from an office

The family picture is on HIS desk.
Ah, a solid, responsible family man.
> The family picture is on HER desk.
> Umm, her family will come before her career.
HIS desk is cluttered.
He's obviously a hard worker and a busy man.
> HER desk is cluttered.
> She's obviously a disorganized scatterbrain.
HE is talking with his co-workers.
He must be discussing the latest deal.
> SHE is talking with her co-workers.
> She must be gossiping.
HE'S not at his desk.
He must be at a meeting.
> SHE'S not at her desk.
> She must be in the ladies' room.
HE'S not in the office.
He's meeting customers.
> SHE'S not in the office.
> She must be out shopping.
HE'S having lunch with the boss.
He's on his way up.
> SHE'S having lunch with the boss.
> They must be having an affair.
The boss criticized HIM.
He'll improve his performance.
> The boss criticized HER.
> *She'll be very upset.*
HE got an unfair deal.
Did he get angry?
> SHE got an unfair deal.
> Did she cry?

HE'S getting married.
He'll get more settled.
    SHE'S getting married.
    She'll get pregnant and leave.
HE'S having a baby.
He'll need a raise.
    SHE'S having a baby.
    She'll cost the company money in maternity benefits.
HE'S going on a business trip.
It's good for his career.
    SHE'S going on a business trip.
    What does her husband say?
HE'S leaving for a better job.
He knows how to recognise a good opportunity.
    SHE'S leaving for a better job.
    Women are not dependable.

4   What is the main idea of the poem? Choose the best sentence.

1 Men are better office workers than women.
2 Married women are unreliable workers.
3 There are different standards for men and women at work.
4 Women are just as ambitious as men in their work.

5   Put these sentences in order.

HE'S an aggressive executive.   She must live alone.
Her poor husband!   HE leaves the office late every evening.
He'll get to the top in no time.   SHE'S an aggressive executive.
He's very hard-working.   SHE leaves the office late every evening.

Can you think of four more lines to continue the poem?

6   In the poem, you may find the lines in italics difficult to understand. Try to put them with their meanings.

1 She'll have a baby and leave.
2 He'll need more money.
3 He'll work better.
4 She'll be very unhappy.
5 Women are unreliable.
6 He must be talking about a recent business agreement.
7 It'll help him to get a better job.

7 **Write down in your own language what these words or phrases mean.**

scatterbrain   gossiping   unfair deal
maternity benefits   opportunity

Use your dictionary to check.

8 **What do you feel about the poem? Is it:**

– funny?   – ironic?   – serious?   – stupid?   – critical?

Do you think that the poet is a woman or a man? Can you say why?
Do you think the attitude to women at work described in the poem is
justified? Have you ever met discrimination towards women in your work?

9 **Here is another poem by the same poet. Read it for your enjoyment.**

Can't do it all!

If I do this
I won't get that done
If I do that
this will slip by
If I do both
neither will be perfect.

Not everything worth doing
is worth doing well.

13 | Getting through

1 This unit is about communication. Look at the photographs. How are the people communicating? Think about their faces, their hands, their eyes, their clothes.

a)

c)

b)

d)

2 What do *you* communicate by your face, your hands, your eyes and your clothes? Do other people agree with you?

3

Look at the title of the passage in exercise 4. Here are the main ideas in the right order.

— speech / most important / communicating
— to talk / be understood by other people / speak a language / use combinations of sounds / stand for / object or idea
— communication / impossible / everyone / own language
— learning a language / very important
— vocabulary of English / not large / 2,000 words / speak / quite well
— words / main thing / communicating
— the way we say the words / important

Can you guess what the passage says?

4

Read and see if you were correct.

Speech

Speech is one of the **most important** ways of **communicating**. It consists of far more than just making noises. **To talk** and also to **be understood by other people**, we have to **speak a language**, that is, we have to **use combinations of sounds** that everyone agrees **stand for** a particular **object or idea. Communication** would be **impossible** if **everyone** made up their **own language**.

Learning a language properly is **very important**. The basic **vocabulary of English** is **not** very **large**, and only about **2,000 words** are needed to **speak** it **quite well**. But the more words you know, the more ideas you can express, and the more precise you can be about their exact meaning.

Words are the **main thing** we use in **communicating** what we want to say. **The way we say the words** is also very **important**. Our tone of voice can express many emotions and shows whether we are pleased or angry, for instance.

5

Fill in the summary with the main ideas.

(1) .... is a very important way of communicating with other people. It is necessary to (2) .... a language to talk to and to understand other people. Learning a (3) .... well is very important. But you only have to know about 2,000 (4) .... to speak (5) .... quite well.

6 Now read this passage about gestures. What is the main idea?

Gestures

As well as talking with our voices we can also talk with our bodies. This may seem surprising at first, but if you watch two people having a conversation you will see that it is true. People often move their hands to emphasise what they are saying and to show the person listening to them that they are saying something important. Listeners use gestures too. They may nod their head to show that they have understood or shake it to indicate disagreement.

Choose the best summary.

1 People often move their hands.
2 We can talk with our bodies.
3 They may nod their head to show that they have understood or shake it to indicate disagreement.

7 Read the next passage which is about body language. Underline the sentence which contains the main idea.

Body language

People also express themselves in the way they walk and in their posture – that is, in the way they carry their body. A self-confident person may well look straight ahead and hold his body erect, whereas a nervous person may stoop slightly and look from side to side. And if you are enjoying talking to someone, you tend to sit forward in your seat. If you are not, you may sit back with your arms folded.

All these body signs are a very important part of communication. This is why actors study them a great deal.

8 *Who* or *what*? Answer the questions about words in the passages.

1 '. . . and only about 2,000 words are needed to speak *it* quite well.' (from Speech). Speak what quite well?

2 '. . . the more precise you can be about *their* exact meaning.' (from Speech). The exact meaning of what?

3 '*This* may seem surprising at first . . .' (from Gestures). What may seem surprising?

4 '. . . two people having a conversation you will see that *it* is true.' (from Gestures). What is true?

5 '. . . that *they* are saying something important.' (from Gestures). Who is saying something important?

6 '*This* is why actors study *them* a great deal.' (from Body Language). What does *This* refer to? And what do actors study?

9 Do you use a lot of gestures when you speak? If so, what kind of gestures? Do some nationalities use more gestures than others? Can you think of any examples?

10 Here is another passage about communication. Read it with a dictionary.

Making sense of what we say

Words are often not enough to make sense in conversation and we use non-verbal ways of getting the message across. When words fail us, gestures often help us out.

Punctuation is an important element in clear message-giving. Written language without punctuation is not easy to follow. Unpunctuated speech is also impossible to follow, so we have a non-verbal system for doing the job.

We use short pauses for commas, longer ones for full stops; a rising and falling pitch (or *vice versa*) for question marks. We accompany words and phrases with small movements of the hands, face and eyes, sentences with movements of the head or an arm, and paragraphs with shifts of the whole body. We use volume and pitch to emphasise words and make meanings clear. For instance, there could be two meanings for a written sentence such as 'They are hunting dogs' but when it is spoken the meaning becomes clear.

Finally, having made our statement in all these ways, we can comment on it, to show whether it is meant to be funny, serious, sarcastic. For instance, a complaint or criticism may be accompanied by a wink or smile which completely changes its meaning.

14 | Dads

The children's quotations and drawings in this unit come from a book called *To Dad*.

1 How do these children see their fathers?

2 Match these sentences with the drawings.

1 Dads grow big hands to spank people.
2 I always feel safe with Dad.
3 My daddy is lazy because he always sits on his bottom.
4 Dads are never working unless they are forced to by mums.
5 Fathers are people who will fight with you but not hurt you.

3 Which quotation do you like best?

1 Fathers are for erning money and helping to keep the human race going.   *(Susan Age 10)*

2 Father's all way's get grey hairs before mother's.   *(Steven Age 10)*

3 A father is a person who let's you do things you're not spos' to.   *(Simon Age 11)*

4 Dads wear socks so that we can not see there hairre legs.   *(Sara)*

5 A dad is a man mum but unlike a mum he is not always on the telephone.   *(Clare)*

6 I really think fathers are a nuisance but you can't do without them.   *(Paul)*

7 A father is a person who drinks about four pints of beer, and next day has a headake.   *(Mark Age 10)*

8 Dads are like moving banks.   *(John Age 11)*

9 The trouble with my dad is that he is ether mad or soft and nice.   *(Guy)*

Can you correct the spelling and punctuation mistakes?

4 Which quotations are about:

- appearance? – discipline? – drinking?
- pocket money? – what dads are for? – what dads are like?

5 Read this passage about the role of the father. Write down three things:

- a modern father does.
- a traditional father does.

The modern father looks after his children
and helps in the house, even if his wife
does not go out to work. The division
between the roles of the mother and the
father is no longer very clear, and dad
does his share of child care: he can change
the baby, dress the children or make the
dinner. This new image of the father is, of
course, completely different from the still
dominant, traditional dad, who represents
authority, is the head of the household and
makes all the 'important' decisions. His wife
is responsible for the domestic side of
family life while he is the one who advises
or punishes as necessary.

What sort of father is yours?

6 What do these words mean? Use your own language.

share dominant authority advises punishes

Check with your dictionary.

7   Read this passage. What sort of father does Beverley have?

What are dads for?

In the home a dad is very important. He is the person who provides us with money to feed and clothe ourselves. He can decorate your bedroom, mend your radio, make cages for your pets, repair a puncture in your bicycle tyre and help you with your maths homework. A dad can be very useful for taking you in the car to and from parties, music lessons, and dancing lessons. A dad is the person whom you ask for pocket money. He is the one who complains about the time you spend talking on the telephone, as he has to pay the bills. Dad is someone who will support you in an argument, if he believes you to be right. He is someone who reads your school report, and treats you if it is good. A dad likes to come into a nice happy home in the evening, and settle back in his chair with a newspaper. He likes to recall his National Service days . . .   *(Beverley, Age 13)*

You can use a dictionary or ask your teacher for help.

8   Which of the things in the passage did your dad do when you were a child?

9   What do you think Beverley would say about mothers? Read the passage again and write a few sentences about mums.

10   In your opinion, what are the roles of a father or a mother? Make a list of the things they should do. Do you think these roles should be different?

15 | What a mistake!

1 This unit is about mistakes. Sometimes people say things which later prove to be quite wrong. Put the two parts of the mistakes together.

1 *'Rail travel at high speed is not possible . . .'*

2 'Animals, which move, have limbs and muscles . . .'

3 *'Far too noisy, my dear Mozart . . .'*

4 'We don't like their sound . . .'

a) 'The earth does not have limbs and muscles; therefore it does not move.'

(Scipio Chiaramonti)

b) *'Groups of guitars are on the way out.'*

(Decca Recording Company when turning down the Beatles in 1962.)

c) 'Far too many notes.'

(The Emperor Ferdinand after the first performance of *The Marriage of Figaro*.)

d) *'Passengers, unable to breathe, would die of asphyxia.'*

(Dr Dionysys Lardner 1793–1859)

What mistake did each person make?

2 Look at the mistakes again. Can you find words that mean:

— refusing? (verb)
— lack of air? (noun)
— legs and arms? (noun)

53

3

These pictures show a very unsuccessful attempt to light a coal fire. Guess the story.

You can use a dictionary or ask your teacher for help.

4   **Here is the story. Put the paragraphs in order. (The pictures will help you.)**

1   He put on his overcoat and approached the car with a bucket of water. But then he fell over a partly-filled petrol can.

2   Seeing what was happening, his neighbour called the *fire brigade*. By the time the *firemen* arrived, Mr Langborne himself was on *fire* with *flames* now leaping freely from his overcoat.

3   On the way out he brushed against a curtain covering the front door. By the time he returned the curtain and the door were both in *flames*.

4   In 1972 Derek Langborne, a scientist, built a *fire* and *lit* it. He then went outside to get some coal. When he returned, he saw that one piece of wood had fallen out and set *fire to* the wood basket. He picked it up and carried it out into the garden.

5   While telephoning the fire brigade, he noticed that the wood basket, which he had put in the garden, had now *set fire to* his car.

What words or phrases helped you?

5   **The words in *italics* are connected with *fire*. Write down in your own language what you think they mean. Check with your dictionary.**

6   **The passage below is a telephone conversation. Put Speaker B's lines into the conversation.**

Speaker A
'Hello, darling. How are you?'
(1) ....
'Don't worry darling. I'm coming right over. I'll feed the children, clean up and cook a dinner your guests will never forget.'
(2) ....
'Dad? . . . Sweetheart, you know Dad died nine years ago.'
(3) ....
'707 5869.'
(4) ....
'Oh no, I dialled the wrong number.'
(5) ....

Speaker B
a)   'You're an angel! How's Dad?'
b)   'Hold on, please. Does this mean you're not coming over?'
c)   'Terrible, Mum. My back is killing me, the children are behaving badly, the house is so untidy – and I'm expecting six guests for dinner.'
d)   'This is 707 5868.'
e)   'What number are you calling?'

7 Read the conversation again and answer the questions:

1 Who are A and B?
2 Who does A think B is?
3 Who does B think A is?
4 How do they realise their mistake?
5 How do you think the conversation finishes? Add three more lines.

8 Everyone makes mistakes but some are more serious than others. Have you ever:

– dialled the wrong number on the telephone and talked to someone you didn't know?
– mistaken a person for someone else?
– taken the wrong train or bus?

Have you ever been in a difficult situation because of a mistake you or somebody else made? Write a few sentences describing it.

9 Can you think of any other things that people believed and which later turned out to be mistakes? Think about:

– the shape of the earth.
– space travel.
– medicine.
– politics.
– entertainers or sportspeople.

16 | Eating out

1 Put the sentences with the cartoons. (There is one extra cartoon!)

1 'Cooeee! We don't like this one either.'
2 'Now you see what comes of drinking the local water.'
3 'Rabbit, Sir?'
4 'An excellent meal. My compliments to the gardener.'

2 Match the parts of the conversation opposite with the lines of pictures in this cartoon.

A — Right then. There's all this left over.
 — Well, just split it six ways. No, three ways.
 — No, Gisèle put the right money in.

 — Well, let's share it between five. That's OK, isn't it?
 — Listen, I paid 50 francs. Don't I get any change, then?
 — Who's just put those ten francs there?

 — OK let's settle it. That's for you, that's for you, and this is for me.
 — What's this? I don't understand. I paid 100 francs. What are these 25 francs?
 — That's what I've just given you.

B — But you just need to split the bill three ways. It isn't difficult!
 — Don't be silly! Just give everyone the same amount.
 — No, because we didn't all pay the same!
 — Let's be sensible about this!

 — But are you stupid or something? I can't believe how difficult Paul's being!
 — Difficult or not, all I know is I paid 100 francs.
 — But Gisèle paid 30 francs, for goodness sake!

 — Look, it's not worth getting upset about. Let's start again. Excuse me,
  could we have six more coffees, please?

C — I've only got a 100 franc note.
 — So have I.
 — Has anybody got the right money?

 — Wait a minute . . . that's too much. Who put in these 30 francs?
 — Me.
 — I paid 100 francs for both of us.
 — Me too.

 — Let's pay and sort it out afterwards. Here you are.
 — Thank you very much, sir.

D — See! It's always Robert who gets the bill!
 — It's because he looks so affluent.

 — Right then, shall we split it six ways?
 — No, not six, we're three couples.
 — Nine carry one . . .

 — Yes, but we've got separate bank accounts.
 — Your private life is none of our business.
 — That makes 163 francs 40 . . .

3 **What are the people in the story like? Here are some useful words.**

friendly	intelligent	kind	hungry	happy	bored
stupid	bad-tempered	calm	shy	sensitive	amusing

4 **What do you know about table manners? Write down five words you may find in the passage.**
Now read and check.

Table manners

The table manners you have in a restaurant are very different from those you have in the home of a friend because, in a restaurant, you can play with your food. If you eat enough expensive meals, and drink enough expensive alcohol in a restaurant, you can do anything. But in the home of a friend, nothing will excuse you for 'restoring' a *Renoir* with potatoes *au gratin*. Playing with food is easy. Here are some things you can do:

— Use mussels as castanets, put bowls over the toes of your shoes and do a flamenco dance on your chair.
— If everyone is having beef dishes, run around the table and try to put the cow back together again.
— Use any roast whole bird as a handpuppet.
— Hang a grilled trout on the wall, or better, stand on the table and use an umbrella and shoelace as a fishing line.

The list is endless. Let imagination rather than taste be your guide.

(From *Modern Manners* by P.J. O'Rourke)

5 **Choose four difficult words from the passage in exercise 4 and ask yourself these questions.**

— What part of speech is the word?
— Do the sentences around the word help you?
— Are there any other words to help you?

Then read on and check. Were you right?

6 **In your opinion, which is the most amusing way of playing with food? Choose from the passage or use your imagination.**

7 Read and find out who *he*, *him* and *his* refer to.

An English tourist was having lunch in a small French restaurant. As the waiter gave *him* his first course, *he* noticed a fly in the vegetable soup. He didn't know very much French, but he called the waiter, pointed at the soup bowl and said, 'Le mouche!' The waiter, who was rather proud of *his* language, replied, 'No, monsieur. La mouche'. 'I say!' said the Englishman, looking very closely at the soup, 'You've got extremely good eyesight'.

8 Find five words which you could leave out of the story. Do not change the general sense. (You cannot cross out two or more words together.)

Example: . . . in a ~~small~~ French restaurant . . .

9 Say what you think of the cartoons.
Does the passage on table manners give good advice?
What can go wrong during a meal in a restaurant?

17 Animal magic

1 The poems in this unit are about animals. Look at the pictures. How do you feel about these animals? Think of five adjectives to describe each one.

Are there any other animals you particularly like or dislike?

2 Read these poems. Put the poems with the animals.

A My dog went mad and bit my hand,
   I was bitten to the bone:
   My wife went walking out with him,
   And then came back alone.

   I smoked my pipe, I nursed my wound,
   I saw them both depart:
   But when my wife came back alone,
   I was bitten to the heart.
   (W.H. Davies)

                B My old cat is dead,
                   Who would butt me with his head,
                   He had the sleekest fur,
                   He had the blackest purr,
                   Always gentle with us
                   Was this black puss.
                   But when I found him today
                   Stiff and cold where he lay
                   His look was a lion's
                   Full of rage, defiance:
                   Oh, he would not pretend
                   That what came was a friend
                   But met it in pure hate.
                   Well died, my old cat.
                   (Hal Summers)

C This is the owl moment I have always known,
   Not yet completely dark,
   When small birds twit him in the park,
   In terror though they tease.
   Out he comes among the trees,
   He comes on oiled wings, alone,
   And mice and tucked-up children hear
   His long too-woo as old as fear.
   (Frances Cornford)

3 Read poem A again. What is the main idea? Choose the best sentence.

1 His dog bit him, so his wife put the dog outside.
2 He was unhappy because his dog went mad and died.
3 He was unhappy because his wife took the dog away to be killed.
4 His dog bit him because it wanted to go for a walk. When it came back it bit him again.

4 **Read poem B again. Are these statements true or false?**

1 It was a friendly, old cat.
2 It was a black cat with beautiful smooth fur.
3 The poet was with the cat when it died.
4 It died quietly.
5 It was a brave cat.
6 The poet admires the way his cat died.

5 **Read poem C again and answer the questions.**

1 What time of day is *the owl moment*?
2 Why are small birds *in terror* of the owl?
3 What do you think *oiled wings* are?
4 How do mice and children feel when they hear the owl?

6 **Read the poems again. Write down the five most important words in each one.**

7 **Can you think of a title for each of the poems?**

8 **What did the poets feel about the animals in their poems?**

affection   admiration   fear   love
remorse   sorrow   sadness respect

9 Read *Who They Are*. Find out who *they* are. What has happened to them?

Who They Are

Wife and husband,
brother and sister,
neighbour and neighbour,
they lie there on the road.
I do not know
who they are
except that they
are dead,
not a whisker twitching.
The cars whizz by not noticing them.
But I do.
Further on the road lies
a bundle
and another bundle.
I do not know
who they are
except that they
are dead,
not a feather stirring.
They used to be able
to run
and fly
across green safe fields.
But now there is a road.
Man has built a motorway.
(Charlotte Harvey)

10 Here are some difficult words. Can you guess what they mean?

whisker   twitch   whizz by   bundle   feather   motorway

Check with your dictionary.

11 Which poem do you like best? Which one do you like least? Why?

12 What animal would you choose to write a poem about? Why? Write down a few words that you would use in a poem about that animal.

18 | Time off

1 Where are these people? What are they doing?

a)

b)

c)

Do you have the same sports and pastimes in your country?

2

The first passage is about holidays and leisure in the USSR. What do you think the passage may say about this? Here are some ideas.

1 Soviet people do not have holidays.
2 They enjoy visiting historical monuments.
3 The arts, especially the theatre, are very popular.
4 Russians enjoy foreign travel.
5 They like to spend their holidays at the seaside.
6 Russians like their leisure activities to be useful.

Can you think of other things people do?

3

Read the passage. Two sentences do not belong in it. Can you find them?

Soviet people take their pleasures seriously. They like to have an *aim*, even when spending the time which is entirely their own. During the summer, people start work very early in the morning so that they can finish early and enjoy a leisurely afternoon. It is difficult to imagine Russians going aimlessly for a walk in the country, though they might go to pick *mushrooms* or *berries*, to visit a place of historical importance, to walk twenty kilometres as a training exercise, or go for a swim at the local beach.

A *feature* of Russian culture which excites admiration is the enjoyment of the arts. All the parks are beautifully kept and are for the use and enjoyment of the people. Quite ordinary people will talk, with obvious delight, about symphony concerts. There is nearly always a *crowd* at the door of the theatre asking for returned tickets.

People in the Soviet Union now have far more leisure time, and more money than ever before. It is therefore possible to spend the weekends in many new ways, and to get away from home for a couple of days. Many people now have over twenty days' holiday a year. This gives an *opportunity* for holidays in the country or at the seaside.

4

Which ideas in exercise 2 did you read about in the passage?

5

What do these words mean in your language?

aim   mushrooms   berries   feature   crowd   opportunity

You can use a dictionary to check.

6 The next passage is about the Chinese and their sports and pastimes. Look at these sentences from the passage and decide where they go.

a) Chinese teams are famous for their skill in table tennis.
b) Here they play cards or Chinese chess, or they attend cultural courses.
c) So many people get up at dawn to do calisthenics in the street.

Chinese people spend one or two evenings a week at workers' cultural palaces run by the commune party committees or by the neighbourhood committees in the towns. The subjects include painting, sculpture, pottery, learning to play musical instruments and singing; all the tutors are experts. There are separate cultural palaces for children, open at weekends.

The Chinese never think of their leisure as time to while away. All their views are heavily influenced by politics, and leisure is seen as time for development, both of mind and body. (Calisthenics are exercises designed to make the body stronger and more graceful.) Again there are experts to instruct, for the Chinese believe in doing everything well.

Sport is also taken seriously. Basketball, volleyball and tennis are also played, and football, a newcomer to Chinese sport, is very popular.

7 How is leisure time different in China from your own country? Write down five things in the passage which do *not* happen in your country.
Example: *In China, people go to workers' cultural palaces.*

8 This passage is about people from the United States of America and their holidays. Read it and find the two types of holiday which they like most.

The most common kind of American holiday is simply to get into the car and drive to a destination such as one of the many national parks, scenic trails, seashores or memorials.

Outdoor recreation may be to go hiking and camping with a tent, or to drive into the wilderness with a 'recreation vehicle' (a large camper), to the distress of those who like their woods quiet.

Americans have always loved foreign travel, but in recent years currency exchange rates which are favourable to the American dollar, and cheaper air fares, mean that more people than ever before can afford their dream of travel abroad.

Europe is the favourite destination for American travellers. Americans enjoy the beautiful old towns, the atmosphere and culture of European cities and the historical buildings far older than any in the USA.

A record number of 5.6 million Americans came to Europe in 1984. Harrods, the London department store, advertises sales in American newspapers like the *New York Times*.

9 Which of these activities are referred to in the passage?

skiing	sightseeing	walking	running
driving	shopping	swimming	camping

10 Which features of free time in the Soviet Union, China and the United States appeal to you?
What are the most popular sports and pastimes in your country? What kinds of holiday are popular?

11 Write a few sentences to answer 1, 2 *or* 3.

1 What sports or pastimes do you enjoy? Is there anything that you would really like to learn to do?
2 How much leisure time do you have each week? How do you spend this time? Are there some things you would like to do but can't because you don't have enough time?
3 Do you think it is important for leisure activities to have a purpose?

19 | The Twenties

This unit is about the Twenties, the years between 1920 and 1930.

1 What can you see in the pictures?

a)

b)

c)
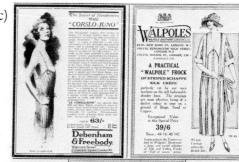

d)

2 Here are the titles of chapters from a book called *The Twenties*. In which chapters would you expect to find the pictures in exercise 1?

    Introduction   Entertainment   School   Clothes
    Fears   Shopping   Transport   Holidays

3 In the passages below, some people are talking about their memories of life in the Twenties. What do you think they might say in each chapter?

4 Put the passages with their chapters.

A 'Life was very different then . . . So different, I can hardly find the words to describe it . . .'

B 'We didn't mind being kept waiting. Time didn't seem to *matter* so much in those days . . . And nowadays, at Sainsbury's, I can tell you it's not much faster. True, you can pick the *goods* up faster, but often you still have to queue to pay at the check-out.'

C 'We are taught to read and do simple arithmetic, but no science and hardly any history or geography.'

D 'I remember all the children, girls as well as boys (in a country school) had enormous great lace-up boots on their feet. Button boots were too grand. There was no such thing as Wellingtons. They wore the same boots in summer. And in those days they didn't *bother* much *about* sizing . . .'

E 'We had one of the first *wirelesses* in the village, because I made it myself when I was about fourteen . . .'

F 'In those days, if you bought a car, the firm you bought it from would often teach you to drive for nothing. You could take as long as you liked. Driving was very different. There was no such thing as yellow lines, and not half the regulations. If you wanted to visit a shop, you *pulled up* in front of it. You stayed as long as you wanted.'

G 'The newspaper was kept strictly away from us. When we were fourteen or fifteen, we still weren't allowed to read about things like that.'

H 'As a child, you could just go straight out and run across the road into the fields and knew you'd be safe. There didn't seem to be the *wickedness* there is now . . .'

I 'Children today seem to have so much freedom in comparison to us. They do so many different things. But we had a happy time, despite everything. People seemed able to *trust* each other. But now, you don't feel safe to go out by yourself at night. It wasn't just because we were living in a village – it was general. I know we*'ve gained* a lot since the Twenties, but we've also lost a lot.'

J 'We never had a holiday when I was young. We couldn't afford it. My honeymoon in Bournemouth was the first . . .'

Underline the words which helped you put the passages with their chapters.

5 Some of the difficult words are in *italics*. Can you put them with their meanings?

  stopped
  everything you have bought
  bad things, bad or dangerous people
  be important
  radios
  believe in people
  care about, take notice of
  things you are going to buy
  have more than before

6 Read each passage again. How do the speakers feel about the past? Can you say which speakers:

  – think that life was better in the Twenties?
  – think that life is better today?
  – are neutral?

7 Which piece of information did you find most interesting?

8 Here are some more pictures. What might the speakers in exercise 4 say about them?

  a)

b)

9   What are the differences between life today and life when you were a child?
Do the changes make life better or worse?

10   What will people remember about the Eighties? Think of photos you have
seen which represent the years between 1980 and 1990.

20 | Mini-sagas

The passages in this unit come from *The Book of Mini-Sagas*. A *mini-saga* is a story which is only 50 words long.

A   He died,
      after 30 years of marriage.
    She, remembering their plan,
     moved to a brave new life,
     miles away beside the sea.
       All seemed idyllic. But
   he had not been there. Soon,
     loneliness tore her apart.
   Sadly she returned to where
      he had been. Still alone,
       she was not lonely.

B   I had been bothered
     with phone calls before
   but none really frightening.
   The phone rang, I picked it
    up and a man's voice said,
       'Time stops at noon.'
  I was worried and decided to
     go down town. I returned
     at noon and entered the
        room, entered the
      room, entered the . . .

C   He was born.
He attended school
at five years old. For
several years he believed
that the heads of mature
dandelions were fairies. He
took piano lessons. He married
and washed his foreign car
every Sunday. After three
score and ten years he
died, but only his
wife noticed.

D   Once upon a time
there was
just Me.
I soon realised there were
three of us, then gradually
four. At last there were just
the two of us. All at once four
of us. Suddenly just the two
of us again. Now there is
only Me
as in the beginning.

1 Read the mini-sagas and choose the best title for each one from this list.

Who made the sun?
Life and numbers
At noon
A walk on the cliffs
Fifty words on the stable and well-balanced life of Mr Average
The happiest days . . .
Love alone need not be lonely
If you were the only girl in the world . . .

2 The mini-sagas all come from different chapters of the book. Which chapter does each one come from?

Domestic	Love	Little weaknesses
The dark fantastic	Miracles	Life and times
Crime and punishment	Twilight years	Politics

You can use a dictionary or ask your teacher for help.

3 Answer the questions about difficult words and phrases.

1 *idyllic:* When she moved away, she soon became lonely. But at first it seemed *idyllic*. Does *idyllic* mean very happy or very sad?

  tore her apart: Loneliness *tore* this woman *apart*. Was this a good or a bad feeling?

2 *bothered:* When you are *bothered* by something, are you likely to be pleased or annoyed?

3 '. . . *he believed that the heads of mature dandelions were fairies.*': What time of the man's life is the writer describing?

4 *score:* A *score* is a certain number like a couple or a dozen. Men and women are supposed to die when they are three score years and ten. How old is *that*?

You can use your dictionary to find the meanings of four more difficult words.

4 Answer the questions.

1 Mini-saga A: a) What is the relationship between *she* and *he*?
  b) Which of these do you think was their plan?
    – When they got old, they would go and live by the sea.
    – If one of them died, the other would move far away and start a new life.
  c) Why did the plan not work?
  d) Does the story have a happy ending?

2 Mini-saga B: Why does the writer repeat the words *entered the room*?

3 Mini-saga C: Which of these words describes the man's life?

  boring   lonely   ordinary
  happy   pointless

  Is the man's life very different from other people's lives?
  How does your life compare with this description?

4 Mini-saga D: Who are *three/two/four of us*? Consider these people:

  mother and father   brothers or sisters
  a girl- or boyfriend   a husband or wife
  children

5 In your own language, write down the *five* most important words in each mini-saga.
Now write down *one* word to describe how you feel after reading each mini-saga.
Which mini-saga do you like most? Why?
Which one do you like least? Why?

6 The sentences of this mini-saga are in the wrong order. Put them in the right order.

Old as his universe

He shook his head.
Perhaps he mistook my meaning.
'How old are you, sir?' I asked.
He appeared extremely ancient, and I approached him slowly, believing him
    to be real.
He smiled with regret, saying 'Fifty words long'.
'Not old.'
The grey beard sat sunning himself.
'How long have you lived?'

7 Look at the chapter headings again. Choose one and think of a suitable subject. Then write a mini-saga of your own. Remember: it must be exactly 50 words long.

Answer key

Unit 1   Soft sell

2 a) 2, 4,   b) 1, 3

3 Put a tiger in your tank: Esso petrol
We'll take more care of you: British Airways
Let your fingers do the walking: Yellow
   Pages Telephone Directory
It's the real thing: Coca Cola

5 In a London Underground train (tube train)
The advert is for the London Underground
but it does not say anything about it.

7 1 the person sitting opposite you in the tube
     train
   2 their first name
   3 the person sitting opposite you; in the
     tube train
   4 the text you are reading, i.e. the
     advertisement

Unit 2   Sleepless nights

2/3 8(d)   3(e)   1(a)   10(f)   6(j)
     2(g)   7(c)   4(b)   9(i)   5(h)

5 Sentence 1

7 1 talk   4 walkers   7 snoring
   2 talking   5 wake up   8 snoring
   3 walk   6 walker   9 snore

Unit 3   Tom's diner

1 √ sitting at a table (both pictures)
   √ pouring coffee (picture (b))
   √ kissing someone (picture (a))
       talking
       eating
   √ hitching up her skirt (picture (a))
   √ reading a newspaper (picture (a))
       looking out of the window
       straightening her stockings
       doing the washing up

2 Some possible answers:

In (a) the woman outside is hitching up her skirt
   but in (b) she is walking by.
In (a) the man behind the counter is kissing a
   girl but in (b) he is pouring coffee.
In (a) the woman at the table is reading a
   newspaper but in (b) she is holding a book.
In (a) it is raining outside but in (b) it is not.

3 Picture (a)

5 1 false   2 false   3 true   4 false
   5 true   6 true   7 true

6 1 *He*: the man behind the counter
     somebody: the woman who comes in
   2 *he*: an actor
   3 *She*: the woman who comes in
   4 *she*: the woman outside
     me: the singer who is sitting at a table
   5 *you*: the woman who comes in
   6 *your*: the person she is thinking about

7 Passage 3

Unit 4   What's your line?

2 1(c) postman   2(a) priest   3(b) storyteller

3 A3   B2   C1

4

Name	Nigel Nice	Sun Jingxiu	Elisabeth Lyneborg
Place	Isle of Skye, UK	Beijing, China	Copenhagen, Denmark
Job	postman	storyteller	priest
Duties	delivers letters and parcels; collects letters from post boxes; passenger service; takes children to school; takes shopping to old people; delivers milk and newspapers and animals	writes and tells stories on street corners; visits schools and cultural centres; teaches moral lessons	runs Sunday school; organises youth club; preaches in two churches; holds social meetings

5 1 true   2 true   3 false   4 true
    5 true   6 false

6 *suburb*: (a)   *preach*: (b)   *recognise*: (c)
    parish: (a)

7 1 storyteller   4 learn what makes
    2 moral   children laugh
    3 other countries   5 learn to talk their
                    language
Other possibilities for 4 and 5 are: listen to
the radio; read a lot.

Unit 5   Poet's corner

1 1 Mr Nobody   2 Honey   3 One day
    4 The Duel

5 Oh, what a thing is a nose!
    It grows and it grows and it grows,
    It grows on your head
    While you're lying in bed
    At the opposite end to your toes.

    ———————————

    It doesn't breathe;
    It doesn't smell;
    It doesn't feel
    So very well.
    I am discouraged
    With my nose:
        The only thing it
        Does is blows.

    (Dorothy Aldis)

Unit 6   Play it safe

2 a)3   b)1   c)2   d)5   e)4

5 Possible answers:
    Burns: matches, hot iron, electric fire
    Scalds: hot water, bath, coffee
    Cuts: broken bottles, windows, glass doors
    Falls: beds, chairs, worktop, table, furniture,
        window, balcony; climbing trees, walls,
        fences
    Drowning: bath, sea

6 1 falls   6 burns   11 drowning
    2 drowning   7 scalds   12 falls
    3 cuts   8 burns   13 burns
    4 scalds   9 cuts   14 drowning
    5 falls   10 cuts   15 scalds

Unit 7   A room with a view

1 1 Room in New York   2 A Passing
    Storm   3 The Dance of Life

2 1(a)   2(c)   3(b)

4 A2   B3   C1

8 The Card Players

Unit 8   Excuses, excuses

4 1(f) 2(h) 3(a) 4(b) 5(d)

7 1(c) 2(b) 3(d) 4(e) 5(a)

8 *man*: the driver   *him*: a judge
he: the driver   *you*: the judge
I: the driver   *her*: the woman
she: a woman

Unit 9   Street furniture

2 You are here: on a street map
Do not walk on the grass: in a park
Queue this side: at a bus stop
Wait: at a pedestrian crossing with traffic
  lights
No collection on Sunday: on a post box

3 1(a) 2(e) 3(d)

4 *protect*: (b)   *rural*: (b)   *erected*: (a)
memorial: (a)

5

	Bus shelters	Public lavatories	Fountains
Why were they built?	to protect people from bad weather	—	to provide people with clean water to drink; as memorials; to persuade people to drink water, not beer or spirits
When were the first ones built?	before the Second World War	in the 1870s	in the nineteenth century
What are they made of?	—	iron, brick, stone	—
What do they look like?	attractive	Indian or Greek temples; cottages; castles	very grand

6 Possible answers:

People wore protective clothing.
Rich local people paid for bus shelters.
People drank a lot of beer and spirits.

Unit 10 How much do you like being with people?

2 *positive:* entertaining, interesting, pleasant, friendly, honest, happy, reliable, relaxed

negative: dull, boring, unhappy, unpleasant, unfriendly, tense, dishonest, uninteresting, unreliable

3 i)6 ii)8 iii)10 iv)1 v)4

5 The endings usually indicate the following parts of speech:
-*y* noun or adjective
-*ly* adverb
-*ily* adverb
-*ed* adjective or past participle
-*ing* adjective or present participle
-*able* adjective

Examples: difficulty, noun; usually, adverb; easily, adverb; interested, adjective; entertaining, adjective; reliable, adjective

6 complicated: extremely shy; keeps himself to himself; fond of humanity; not at ease with people

Unit 11 Brainteasers

1 1 Malta, India
2 Panama, Spain
3 Peru, Uganda
4 Sweden, Lebanon;
5 Chad, Andorra

2 1 Forgive your enemies but never forget their names.
2 Wagner has some wonderful moments but some awful half hours.
3 Early to bed and early to rise makes a man healthy, wealthy and dead.
4 Middle age is when your age begins to show around your middle.

3 1k, 2j, 3f, 4c, 5l, 6e, 7a, 8h, 9b, 10d, 11g, 12i

5 A farmer was asked how many animals he had. He answered, 'They're all horses except for two, all sheep except for two and all pigs except for two.' How many animals did he have? (Answer: 3)

A son asked his father how old he was and the father replied, 'Your age is now one quarter of mine, but five years ago it was only one fifth.' How old is the father? (Answer: 80)

6 1 $46\frac{2}{3}$ days
2 The Countess is Lady Constance's mother.
3 First you fill the three-litre container. Empty it into the five-litre container. Fill the three-litre container again and empty it into the five-litre container until it is full. Now one litre will remain in the three-litre container.
4 9.30
5 49
6 Johnny who saw the smoke knew of it first; Bobby who heard the shot, second; and Willie who saw the bullet hit the water, third. Light travels faster than sound and sound faster than a bullet.

7 1

Name	Hobby
John Greene	fishing
Bobby Smith	golf
Andy Sheene	swimming
David Brown	bowling
Peter Rolfe	canoeing

2

Name	Colour of hair	Occupation
Bernice	redhead	typist
Amelia	brunette	receptionist
Caroline	blonde	hairdresser

Unit 12 Women at work

3 Picture D

4 There are different standards for men and women at work.

5 HE'S an aggressive executive.
He'll get to the top in no time.
    SHE'S an aggressive executive.
    Her poor husband!
HE leaves the office late every evening.
He's very hard working.
    SHE leaves the office late every evening.
    She must live alone.

6 1 She'll get pregnant and leave.
2 He'll need a raise.
3 He'll improve his performance.
4 She'll be very upset.
5 Women are not dependable.
6 He must be discussing the latest deal.
7 It's good for his career.

Unit 13   Getting through

5 1 Speech   2 speak   3 language
4 words   5 it

6 2

7 The first sentence of the passage contains the main idea.

8 1 English; 2 words; 3 the idea that we can talk with our bodies; 4 the idea that we can talk with our bodies; 5 people; 6 This refers to the fact that body signs are an important part of communication. Actors study body signs.

Unit 14   Dads

2 1(e)   2(a)   3(c)   4(d)   5(b)

3 *spelling:* earning, always, supposed, their, hairy, headache, either
punctuation: Fathers, always, mothers

4 *appearance:* 2, 4   *discipline:* 3
drinking: 7   *pocket money:* 8
what dads are for: 6
what dads are like: 5, 9

5 Suggested answers:

a modern father: looks after the children, helps in the house, changes the baby, dresses the children, makes dinner

a traditional father: represents authority, makes the important decisions, advises or punishes as necessary

Unit 15   What a mistake!

1 1(d)   2(a)   3(c)   4(b)

2 *refusing:* turning down
lack of air: asphyxia
legs and arms: limbs

4 4   3   5   1   2

6 1(c)   2(a)   3(e)   4(d)   5(b)

7 1 a mother and a daughter.
2 A thinks B is her daughter.
3 B thinks A is her mother.
4 B asks about her father but A's husband is dead.

Unit 16   Eating out

1 1(e)   2(a)   3(c)   4(d)

2 1D   2C   3A   4B

7 *he:* English tourist
him: English tourist
his: the French waiter

8 vegetable, very, soup, rather, very, extremely

Unit 17   Animal magic

2 A: dog   B: cat   C: owl

3 3

4 1 true   3 false   5 true
2 true   4 false   6 true

5 1 at nightfall
2 because it hunts them for food
3 silent wings
4 frightened

9 *they:* the animals and birds killed by cars on the motorway

Unit 18   Time off

1 a) USA; playing baseball
  b) Russia; playing chess
  c) China; playing cards

3 During the summer people start work very
  early in the morning so that they can finish
  early and enjoy a leisurely afternoon.
  All the parks are beautifully kept and are for
  the use and enjoyment of the people.

4 2 3 5 6

6 . . . in the towns. (b) The subjects include . . .
  . . . mind and body. (c) Calisthenics . . .
  . . . taken seriously. (a) Basketball . . .

9 outdoor holidays and foreign holidays

10 camping, sightseeing, driving, walking,
   shopping

Unit 19   The Twenties

2 a): Entertainment
  b): Transport
  c): Clothes (or Shopping)
  d): Shopping (or Clothes)

4 A: Introduction   F: Transport
  B: Shopping   G: Entertainment
  C: School   H: Fears
  D: Clothes   I: Fears
  E: Entertainment   J: Holidays

5 *stopped:* pulled up
  everything you have bought: your stuff
  bad things, bad or dangerous people:
    wickedness
  be important: matter
  radios: wirelesses
  believe in people: trust
  care about, take notice of: bother about
  things you are going to buy: goods
  have more than before: 've gained

6 *Better in the Twenties:* B, H, I, F
  Better today: D, G, J, C
  Neutral: A, E

Unit 20   Mini-sagas

1 A Love alone need not be lonely
  B At noon
  C Fifty words on the stable and well-
    balanced life of Mr Average
  D Life and numbers

2 A Love
  B The dark fantastic
  C Domestic or Life and times
  D Domestic

3 1 *idyllic*: very happy   *tore her apart*: a
    bad feeling
  2 *bothered*: annoyed
  3 his childhood
  4 70

4 A: A woman and her dead husband
      If one of them died, the other would
        move far away and start a new life.
      Because she was lonely where he had
        never lived.
      Yes, because she was no longer lonely.

  B: Because time has stopped at noon.

  D: *three:* the writer, with mother and father
      four: the writer, with mother and father
        and a brother or a sister
      two: the writer and wife/husband
      four: the writer, with wife/husband and
        two children

6 The grey beard sat sunning himself.
  He appeared extremely ancient, and I
    approached him slowly, believing him to
    be real.
  'How old are you sir?' I asked.
    He shook his head.
  'Not old.'
    Perhaps he mistook my meaning.
  'How long have you lived?'
    He smiled with regret, saying 'Fifty words
    long.'

To the teacher

The primary aim of *Reading 1* is to help the learner develop the skill of reading English. The means of achieving this aim are many, but probably the most important is *learner motivation*. Reading in the mother tongue is such an enjoyable activity that it would seem highly desirable to recreate this enjoyment when the student starts to read in the foreign language. But the motivation to read in the mother tongue may often be different from the motivation to read in the foreign tongue.

The reader in the mother tongue has a reason for reading and the consequent motivation is self-directed. The reason may sometimes be spurious or ephemeral, but at least this reader is in control and can choose what he or she wants to read. But in the foreign language reading is often a classroom activity and may be directed and controlled by the teacher. This reader is often told either implicitly or explicitly what to read and how. So how does the teacher in the artificial situation of the classroom recreate the motivation for, and enjoyment of reading that the reader would normally experience in real-life?

There seem to be three key factors in stimulating the learner's motivation: the text, the task and the teacher's role. In *Reading 1* we have tried to incorporate these three factors in an attempt to make reading enjoyable and motivating.

The text

The type of texts we choose for use in the classroom has an obvious and important role to play in stimulating learner motivation. We have tried to choose material which will be varied, interesting and intellectually stimulating to as many people as possible. It does not seem a satisfactory way of promoting motivation to use material which contains familiar ideas and information and in which the only interest is in deciphering the foreign language.

Many of the texts contain some vocabulary which will be unfamiliar to the learner. When we were selecting the texts, it seemed important to us to use as much authentic material as possible, that is to say, material which was not specially written for language learners. We feel that the learner should be exposed to real-life, roughly graded English at as early a stage as possible. We have avoided all carefully graded texts which would pose little or no comprehension difficulties and which would not necessarily develop the learner's reading skills.

Motivation through the text and its content was a primary objective. But realistically, it seems unlikely that a text will interest all of the people all of the time. Another factor seems essential in stimulating motivation: the task.

The task

The tasks or activities which accompany the texts in *Reading 1* have two intentions: the first is to create or maintain learner motivation; the second is to develop the useful microskills for reading.

We have already said that a text and its content will rarely be able to bear the full responsibility for stimulating genuine learner motivation. But if it is accompanied by interesting tasks, we feel that learner motivation can be created and maintained artificially. The classroom context remains artificial and few of the tasks in *Reading 1* could be said to be real-life tasks; we do not usually have to match headings, pictures and paragraphs, or unscramble sentences when we read a novel or a magazine! Yet these kinds of tasks may be problem-solving activities or stimuli for discussion; they are not always linguistically complex, but are often conceptually difficult, and therefore enjoyable and motivating in their own right.

The microskills for reading which are presented in *Reading 1* are developed using a variety of different activity types.

Extracting main ideas   It is important to help the learner look for the main ideas of a passage and to avoid getting distracted by unfamiliar vocabulary. Typical activity types which develop this skill are matching exercises: text with picture, text with heading etc. Sometimes, there may be an extra sentence, or an extra picture. This only makes the reader think a bit more!

Understanding text organisation   It is sometimes difficult to understand what information is important in a passage and where it should come. Text organisation activities help the reader to see what belongs to a passage, and how sentences are joined together in a logical way.

Inferring   A writer may want you to understand more than the actual words you read. Inferring activities draw the reader's attention to the overall atmosphere of the passage. It also helps build their vocabulary.

Predicting   Before a learner reads a text, it may be helpful to encourage them to look at the subject or the title of the passage, and to think about the possible content. But remember: it does not matter if the learner fails to predict correctly. The activity still helps prepare them for reading.

Dealing with unfamiliar words   In this book there will be many words which the learner will not understand. This is because all the passages are examples of real-life written English. It is important to try and guess the general sense of a difficult word, and there are a number of activities which help them deal with unfamiliar vocabulary without using dictionaries or asking the teacher to explain or translate.

Reading for specific information   We sometimes read to find the answer to a particular question, and not to understand the general sense of the passage. There are a number of exercises like this to help the learner read for specific information.

Linking ideas   Often a writer uses several different words to describe the same idea. Sometimes the use of a pronoun, for example, may be confusing, although the context usually makes the meaning clear. This type of exercise concentrates on the words used to link ideas.

However, it has to be said that one disadvantage of giving too much importance to microskills is that the learner may already have acquired some or all of them. In this case the importance of the first intention of these tasks should be born in mind.

The teacher's role

Motivation is a most elusive factor in learning: we know it facilitates learning, but we do not quite know how to stimulate it, even though we all know for sure when we are addressing motivated learners. Our attempt in *Reading 1* has been to use as many different texts and tasks as possible to achieve this. But ultimately the teacher has the final responsibility in making sure the learner remains happy and interested in his or her work by using the teaching material in general and *Reading 1* in particular, flexibly and intuitively. As a teacher using this book, you can:

– either work through each unit in order or choose only those which are likely to interest your students. You may not have time to do every unit, and not every unit will interest everyone.
– either do every exercise, or only do those which are useful or interesting to the students.
– either start at the beginning of the book and work through to the end, or choose to do units in random order. There is no particular grading in the book, although the texts at the beginning tend to be linguistically less complex than those at the end.
– let the students work alone, or in pairs.
– let the students choose the texts which interest them, or direct them to particular units.
– choose units which cover language points or themes that are related to the main syllabus of your course.
– extend the work covered in the unit with further discussion or writing practice.
– help learners to read actively by avoiding translating or explaining every single item of vocabulary which they do not understand.

Finally, remember that this book is designed to help you teach, and to help your learners learn. It is a framework for reading practice, and not a straitjacket. Do not hesitate to adapt the material if you so choose.
We hope you and your students enjoy using *Reading 1*.

Acknowledgements

The authors and publishers are grateful to the following:

The Ford Motor Company Ltd and The Rover Group plc for the advertisements on p. 1; Jeremy Pembrey for the photographs on pp. 3, 30 (a), (c) (d) and (e), 33 and 45; les Karamasov and Elm Tree Books for the cartoon and captions on pp. 4 and 5 from *Sleepless Nights*; AGF Music Ltd / Waifersongs Ltd for the lyrics on p. 8 (© 1987 AGF Music Ltd / Waifersongs Ltd. Lyrics used with permission, all rights reserved); Wayland Publishers Ltd for the photographs on p. 10 (a) and (c), and the extracts on p. 11 from *We Live in Britain*, *We Live in Denmark* and *We Live in China*; Sally and Richard Greenhill for the photographs (b) on p. 10 and (c) on p. 66; the Scottish Health Education Council for the pictures on p. 17 and the extracts on pp. 18 and 19; Punch for the cartoon on p. 20; Sheldon Memorial Art Gallery, University of Nebraska-Lincoln for the painting 'Room in New York' by Edward Hopper on p. 21; The Beaverbrook Art Gallery, Fredericton, N.B., Canada for the painting on p. 21 by J.J.J. Tissot (1836–1902) 'A Passing Storm' (oil on canvas, 76.8 × 99.7 cm.), gift of the Sir James Dunn Foundation; The Nasjonalgalleriet, Oslo for the painting on p. 21 'The Dance of Life' by Edvard Munch; Her Majesty the Queen for Gracious Permission to reproduce the painting 'The Card Players' by De Hooch on p. 24; Unwin Hyman Ltd for their kind permission to reproduce the extracts taken from *Excuses, Excuses* by Gordon Wood and Ernie Daniels; The Bodley Head for the extracts on p. 31 from *Street Furniture* by Kenneth Hudson; Adams Picture Library for picture (b) on p. 30; Phoebus Publishing Company / BPC Publishing Ltd and The Reader's Digest for the questionnaire on pp. 34/35; Octopus Publishing Group plc for extracts from *Brainteasers and Puzzles* by Giles Brandreth on pp. 37–40; W.H. Allen for the poems on pp. 42–44 from *Is This Where I Was Going?* by Natasha Josefowitz; Exley Publications Ltd for the drawings on p. 49 by James, Orsina, Bilge, Scott and Harold, and for the quotations on p. 49 by Scott, Anne Fowka, Billie, Christine Johnston and David, and for the quotations on p. 50, all from *To Dad* edited by Richard and Helen Exley; Claire Bretécher for her cartoon on p. 58; Grafton Books for the extracts from *Modern Manners* by P.J. O'Rourke on p. 60; Bruce Coleman Ltd for the photographs on p. 62; Jonathan Cape Ltd and the University of New England for the poem 'D for Dog' by W.H. Davies © 1963 by Jonathan Cape Ltd, reprinted from *The Complete Poems of W.H. Davies*; Oxford University Press for the poem by Hal Summers on p. 63, © Hal Summers 1978, reprinted from *Tomorrow is My Love* by Hal Summers; Christopher Cornford for the poem by Frances Cornford on p. 63; Charlotte Harvey for her poem on p. 65; John Massey Stewart for the photograph (b) on p. 66; Paul Popper Ltd for photographs (a) on p. 66 and (b) and (d) on p. 70; Simon and Schuster Young Books, Hemel Hempstead, U.K. for permission to reproduce the extracts on pp. 67–69 from *The Soviet Union*, *China* and *The USA*, titles in the series Macdonald's Countries; The Illustrated London News for pictures (a) and (c) on p. 70 and (a) on p. 72; Mary Evans Picture Library for the photograph on p. 73; A. & C. Black (Publishers) Ltd for the extracts on p. 71 from *Young in the Twenties* by Eleanor Allen; Alan Sutton Publishing Ltd, Gloucester and The Daily Telegraph plc for the extracts on pp. 74, 75 and 77 from *The Book of Mini-Sagas*.

It has not been possible to identify the sources of all the material used and in such cases the publishers would welcome information from copyright owners.

Illustrations drawn by Lynda Arnold, Tony Hall, Chris Pavely, Trevor Ridley, Chris Rothero and Shaun Williams.
Artwork by Hardlines.
Book design by Peter Ducker MSTD